REAL LIFE ISSUES

# COPING WITH
# DOMESTIC VIOLENCE

**Liz Miles**

**www.raintreepublishers.co.uk**
Visit our website to find out more information about Raintree books.

**To order:**
☎ Phone 0845 6044371
▤ Fax +44 (0) 1865 312263
✉ Email myorders@raintreepublishers.co.uk

Customers from outside the UK please telephone +44 1865 312262

©Raintree is an imprint of Capstone Global Library Limited, a company incorporated in England and Wales having its registered office at 7 Pilgrim Street, London, EC4V 6LB – Registered company number: 6695582

Text © Capstone Global Library Limited 2011
First published in hardback in 2011
First published in paperback in 2012

Edited by Louise Galpine and Laura Knowles
Designed by Richard Parker
Picture research by Liz Alexander
Originated by Capstone Global Library Ltd
Printed and bound in China by South China Printing Company Ltd

ISBN 978 1 406 21988 3 (hardback)
14 13 12 11 10
10 9 8 7 6 5 4 3 2 1

ISBN 978 1 406 21995 1 (paperback)
15 14 13 12 11
10 9 8 7 6 5 4 3 2 1

**British Library Cataloguing in Publication Data**
Miles, Liz.
Coping with domestic violence. -- (Real life issues)
362.8'292-dc22
A full catalogue record for this book is available from the British Library.

**Acknowledgements**
We would like to thank the following for permission to reproduce photographs: © Capstone Publishers p. 30 (Karon Dubke); Alamy pp. 10 (© www.Beepstock.com/Robinbeckham), 12 (© Picture Partners), 18 (© Martyn Vickery), 21 (© Chris Rout), 25 (© Hatonthestove), 26 (© Gabe Palmer), 28 (© UK Stock Images Ltd), 34 (© Angela Hampton Picture Library), 15 (© Richard Church), 43 (© MBI), Corbis pp. 11 (© Gerard Launet/PhotoAlto), 16 (© Roy Morsch), 22 (© Ghislain & Marie David de Lossy/cultura); Getty Images pp. 23 (Jason Merritt), 27 (Steven Puetzer/Photographer's Choice), 29 (Peter Dazeley/The Image Bank), 37 (Andy Lee/First Light), 39 (Priscilla Coleman), 41 (David Perez Shadi/Taxi); Photolibrary pp. 4 (Enrique Algarra/age fotostock), 5 (Dave L. Ryan/Index Stock Imagery), 33 (Cade Martin/Uppercut Images), 35 (Radius Images); Press Association Images p. 38 (Siddharth Darshan Kumar/AP); Rex Features p. 9 (BURGER/Phanie); Science Photo Library p. 14 (DR P. MARAZZI); Shutterstock p. 6 (© ejwhite).

"Distressed texture" design detail reproduced with permission of iStockphoto/© Diana Walters.

Cover photograph of a girl reproduced with permission of iStockphoto/© Shelly Perry.

Extracts on pages 8, 24, 32 and 36 are from *Children's Perspectives on Domestic Violence*, Audrey Mullender et al. (Sage, 2002)

We would like to thank Anne Pezalla for her invaluable help in the preparation of this book.

Every effort has been made to contact copyright holders of material reproduced in this book. Any omissions will be rectified in subsequent printings if notice is given to the publishers.

**Disclaimer**

# CONTENTS

**Stay safe on the internet!**
When you are on the internet, never give personal details such as your real name, phone number, or address to anyone you have only had contact with online. If you are contacted by anyone who makes you feel uncomfortable or upset, don't reply to them, tell an adult, and block that person from contacting you again.

Any words appearing in the text in bold, **like this**, are explained in the glossary.

# Introduction

Domestic violence is when family members or people in a relationship repeatedly treat each other very badly. The **abuse** can be **physical** (such as hitting) or **emotional** (such as calling you names to upset you). Both types of abuse are hurtful. Because of the different types of domestic violence, the term "domestic abuse" is sometimes used instead of domestic violence.

## Where?

Domestic violence takes place in the family home or in places the family visit. Often, no one else knows it is going on. It is kept a secret.

Abuse can be physical, verbal, or emotional, but no type of abuse is ever acceptable.

## Who?

Domestic violence can happen between adults, such as a mother and father, or between younger people, such as brothers and sisters. It may also involve an adult or even an older brother or sister being violent to children. Violence towards children is called **child abuse**. Domestic violence tends to happen mostly between men and women, with the man being violent towards the woman. However, women abuse men sometimes, too.

## Say "No!"

Abuse causes all kinds of feelings in the **victim**, such as sadness, fear, and anger. It is important for people to get help if they are experiencing abuse or violence. Nobody should have to accept being abused. This book will explain how and where to get help.

Domestic violence can continue for many years in a family home.

# Your rights

Domestic violence is wrong. There is no excuse for **abuse** and the **victim** is never responsible. It should never happen, yet it does happen all around the world.

Everyone has the right to be treated with respect. There is no excuse for domestic violence.

## Online!

Every human being has a right to be respected and treated well. International laws and agreements protect human rights. An **abuser** is not respecting the rights of their **victim**. You can find out about your rights by viewing the Convention on the Rights of the Child online (see page 46).

# Children's rights

Children have the right to be well looked after by the adults who care for them. The adults' duty is called their parental responsibility. If parents or **carers neglect** or treat children badly, they can be taken to **court**. Just as violence towards children is a form of abuse, so is neglect.

# Is it a crime?

There is no single **criminal offence** covering domestic violence. This is because there are many different types of abuse. However, many of the things that **abusers** do are crimes. For example, making people frightened of violence, and actual **assault** and wounding are all criminal offences. If you are being abused it helps to remember that the law is there to help you.

## BEHIND THE HEADLINES

The charity UNICEF tries to protect children. For example, in its 2010 Humanitarian Action report it said it needed £24,069,000 for child protection around the world. This included money to help governments prevent **child abuse** in their countries.

# Types of domestic violence

There are many different forms of domestic violence. Most are to do with one person having power over another. The **abuser** hurts the **victim** in some way, making them feel miserable, worthless, and powerless. By making the victim feel weak, the abuser feels that he or she can gain more control.

## Verbal abuse

Shouting is a form of **verbal abuse**. Verbal abuse can control, mock, embarrass, threaten, and upset the victim. If someone shouts at you it is shocking and can make you feel angry and upset. Constant yelling, threats, and swearing are frightening. You may fear you will be **physically** harmed next. Don't put up with verbal abuse from abusers – tell them to stop and ask them to say sorry.

Abusers can use criticism to hurt their victims. This might include telling them they are useless, or embarrassing them in front of other people. Not talking or replying to someone is also a form of verbal abuse. To be left out and ignored can be as hurtful as being shouted at.

## CASE STUDY

Constant shouting is often a part of threatening behaviour. A 16-year-old girl remembers the shouting that came with abuse: "It was the worst part of my life – constantly being shouted at, frightened, living in fear. You will never know what it was like, thinking that every day could be your last." An 8-year-old girl remembers threats: "He used to say, 'I am going to kill you at night-time when you are asleep.' … I used to get very frightened." Some children are unwilling to talk about their experiences so publicly.

An abuser may use verbal threats. This is unacceptable behaviour.

## Emotional abuse

You may feel you are being abused, even though the abuser is not actually saying anything abusive or hitting you. There are many forms of abuse which are not obvious but which can affect your emotions.

## Control

Controlling other people's lives is a form of **emotional** abuse. A husband in the family might take control of all the money, so no one else can make decisions about what to buy. A mother may have to ask for money just to buy food. She might have to explain every penny she has spent. The abuser might insist on making *all* the family decisions. This is abusive and unfair. Family decisions should be discussed. If you feel that someone is too controlling in your home, talk to an adult you trust.

Abused children often feel alone.

## Isolation

Some abusers **isolate** their victims so that it is harder for them to get help. They might stop the victim from seeing friends or relatives, stop them from using the telephone, and shut them up in the house.

### CASE STUDY

Imprisonment is an extreme case of control. In 2010, a 14-year-old American girl was locked in her bathroom for nearly two months by her father. She had to sleep on a blanket and was given very little to eat. Luckily, she escaped through the attic, and raced off on her bike. She went to a coffee shop, where an adult called the police. Her father and stepmother were arrested for **child abuse**, kidnapping, and **unlawful imprisonment**. The brave girl is now safe.

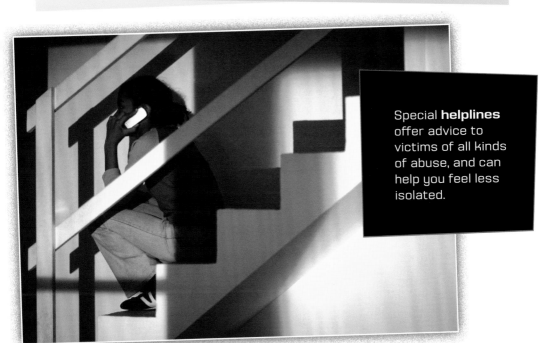

Special **helplines** offer advice to victims of all kinds of abuse, and can help you feel less isolated.

Hearing violence between parents, such as shouting and screaming, and plates crashing, is very frightening. If you witness violence like this, try to talk about it to an adult you can trust.

# Physical abuse

Physical violence involves a person physically hurting another person, such as pushing, hitting, punching, kicking, or pinching someone. It can also involve throwing objects. Thousands of children **witness** physical violence or are a victim of it. Many people and charities are trying to stop it. If you witness violence, don't risk getting involved by trying to stop it yourself. Instead, get help from an adult or by phoning the police.

## CASE STUDY

A girl, aged 10, had to leave home with her mother to escape from domestic violence. Her father was hitting her mother every day. They were glad to get away, yet it seemed unfair that they had to leave their home – when it was the father who was the violent one.

# Child sexual abuse

**Sexual** abuse is when someone makes you feel uncomfortable by touching or looking at you in ways that are overly personal or rude. A sexual abuser can also make you feel uncomfortable in other ways too, such as by showing you private parts of his or her body. If this happens to you, you should tell an adult you trust. It is wrong. It is not your fault and it should be stopped.

# Crossing the line

Sometimes children are not sure whether they are being **abused** or not, or whether what is happening to them is normal or wrong. **Abusers** may tell their children that the abuse is a punishment, and that they deserve it because they have misbehaved. However, it is important to remember that no one has the right to hurt you, or to make you feel scared. All forms of abuse are wrong, and there is never any excuse.

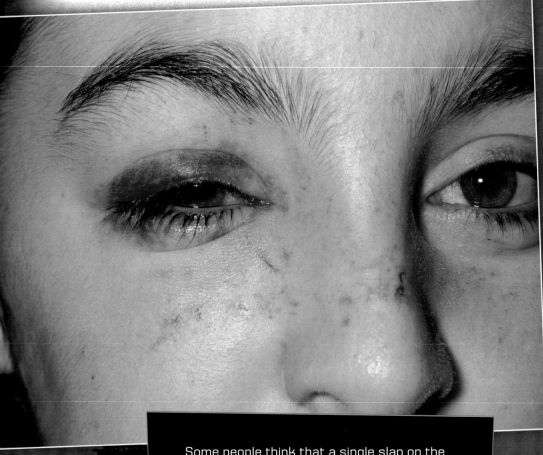

Some people think that a single slap on the leg is okay to discipline a child. However, to hit or slap a child hard or repeatedly is wrong, and is likely to be abuse.

# False reports

It is unfair to report domestic violence to the police if it isn't happening. But if you are worried about how you are being treated and you are not sure if it is abuse or not, you must talk to an adult you trust, such as your teacher. It's important to tell someone how you feel.

Parents must teach their children right from wrong. They have the right to discipline their children for bad behaviour. But they do not have the right to hurt them.

## Online!

Abusers can use mobile phones to control their **victims** or to abuse them in other ways. To find out more, go to the Safe Space website (see page 47). If someone is using your mobile phone to abuse or control you, look at the list of suggestions on what you can do.

Mobile phones help you keep in touch and stay safe, but they can also be used by abusers to control their victims.

15

# Teen violence

Domestic violence between young people is thought to be increasing. In the United Kingdom, 25 per cent of teenage girls suffer **physical** violence from their boyfriends, such as being slapped, punched, or beaten.

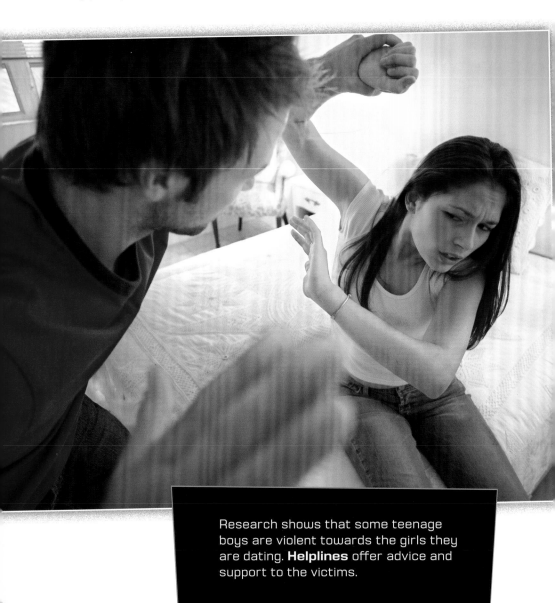

Research shows that some teenage boys are violent towards the girls they are dating. **Helplines** offer advice and support to the victims.

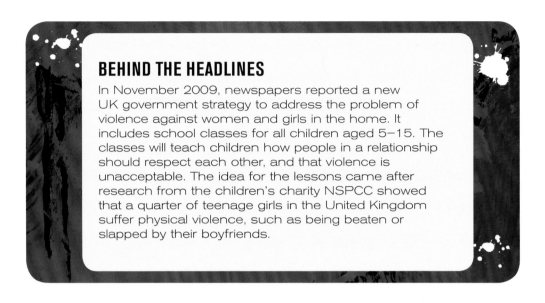

## BEHIND THE HEADLINES

In November 2009, newspapers reported a new UK government strategy to address the problem of violence against women and girls in the home. It includes school classes for all children aged 5–15. The classes will teach children how people in a relationship should respect each other, and that violence is unacceptable. The idea for the lessons came after research from the children's charity NSPCC showed that a quarter of teenage girls in the United Kingdom suffer physical violence, such as being beaten or slapped by their boyfriends.

# Awareness

In 2010 the US Senate decided to extend a Teen Dating Violence Awareness and Prevention Week into a National Teen Dating Violence Awareness and Prevention Month, which will take place every February. The decision to have an awareness month focusing on this issue was made because research showed that one in three adolescent girls in the United States is a victim of physical, emotional, or verbal abuse from a dating partner.

Making parents and schools more aware of the violence between dating teens is important. If people don't know violence is happening, how can they help? If you are worried that a teenager is a victim of violence, talk to an adult you can trust.

# Violence towards women

Some women are violent towards men, but most domestic violence involves men attacking women. A survey in the United Kingdom showed that 89 per cent of victims of **ongoing** domestic violence between adults were women. Unfortunately, some people think that violence towards women is not as bad as it is. Many people don't understand that the victims need help.

If your mum is being abused give her lots of love and try to encourage her to get help. Sometimes she may not be able to think clearly because she is so upset.

If you **witness** violence between your parents or carers, talk to an adult or ring a helpline. It is upsetting to see and you will

# Myths

Here are some myths about violence against women:

- "Some women deserve it."
  WRONG: no one deserves to be abused. All forms of domestic abuse are bad.

- "It's not his fault he's violent – he just can't control his temper."
  WRONG: a loss of temper is no excuse. Anger is a natural feeling but violence is not an acceptable way of showing your feelings.

- "Emotional abuse isn't domestic violence."
  WRONG: just like being hit, emotional abuse hurts the victim and is dangerous and damaging.

## WHAT DO YOU THINK?

When the Australian government ran a campaign called "violence against women: Australia says no", a few people argued that it was unfair to focus the campaign on men being violent to women. What do you think? Does the focus of the campaign sound like a good idea?

| The campaign was fair | The campaign was unfair |
|---|---|
| The majority of domestic violence is carried out by men towards women. | Men are victims of domestic violence too. Campaigns should be against all domestic violence. |
| Domestic violence is a serious issue. Any campaign that raises awareness of the problem is a good thing. | Some men might not report being victims of domestic violence because they feel embarrassed or think people won't believe them. Campaigns like this one don't help. |

# Fears and worries

It is very upsetting to see someone being **abused** in your home. If you **witness** domestic abuse you probably feel all kinds of emotions, such as fear, anger, and loneliness. All these feelings are natural. However, it is important to remember that the abuse is not your fault, and that it can be stopped.

## Children's advice

It helps to know how other children have coped. Many children who have experienced domestic violence have good advice to give. For example, one group suggested that it is important to stay calm, and think things through. Once you are calm, it is easier to decide what to do to sort the problem out.

## Online!

When facing violence in your life, understanding your own feelings is important. Looking on the internet for advice can help, too. For example, the Refuge website reminds you of important points, such as the fact that any abuse is not your fault and that hitting is against the law. It explains that it is best not to try to stop any violence yourself or to protect someone, or you could get hurt. If you witness violence, it is best to get help. Visit Refuge's website (see page 47) for useful advice about dealing with domestic violence.

Worries at home can make you feel unwell. Some children cannot sleep, while others might get a stomach ache. Feeling like this means it is time to get help.

# Common worries

Sometimes children are **physically** attacked by their mother or father, or by another relative. Sometimes the abuse might take another form. Whatever type of abuse it is, it can feel terrifying to the **victim**. It causes all sorts of worries and problems.

Children often worry that being abused is their own fault. This is not true. It is always the **abuser's** fault, not the child's. Children also worry that they will be made to feel embarrassed if they say anything. In fact, abuse is only embarrassing for the abuser. Children should never feel ashamed, and should always tell someone if they are being abused. It is hard to tell someone that the person you love, or once loved, is hurting you. But whoever the abuser is, the abuse must be stopped.

Telling someone about abuse often brings on a feeling of great relief.

Rihanna was abused by her boyfriend. Her story was in many newspapers, so it made people more aware of how victims feel.

## CASE STUDY

Victims of violence often feel alone, as if they are the only person being abused. Singer Rihanna was interviewed about her ex-boyfriend attacking her. She explained how it can happen to anyone. She also reminded us that abuse is not the victim's fault. She said, "This happened to me. I didn't cause this. I didn't do it."

## Love and hate

It is confusing when the abuser is someone the child loves, such as his or her father. However, no matter how much the child cares for the abuser, the kindest thing to do is to get help. Stopping the abuse is good, for both the victim and the abuser. Ringing a **helpline** is a useful first step.

# Steps to safety

There are many ways to stop the cycle of domestic violence in a home. Every year thousands of families receive help, and the **abuse** stops.

## It isn't always easy to leave

**Victims** might find it difficult to take steps to get help or to escape their **abuser**. Some of the reasons are:

- fear of being attacked if they leave
- feeling it's their fault and having low **self-esteem**
- worries about money and how they will support themselves and their families alone
- not having friends or knowing where to go for help.

If you know someone who is being abused, you can help support that person by encouraging him or her to tell other adults about the abuse.

## CASE STUDY

During a group interview, children explained: "Grown-ups think they should hide it and shouldn't tell us, but we want to know. We want our mums … to talk to us about what they are going to do – we could help make decisions."

Many abused people feel too ashamed to get help. It is the abuser's fault that they feel like this.

## What to do

If you **witness** abuse at home, you can start to find a way out by following this advice:

- Tell someone about the abuse. If possible, talk to the person being hurt.
- Talk to a teacher, neighbour, friend, or friend's parent. Choose someone you can trust.
- If you want to get advice without anyone knowing, you can contact a professional through a telephone **helpline** or the internet.

**25**

# Who to tell?

Whether you are a witness to domestic violence or a victim, there are many professional, caring people to talk to. You might prefer to talk to another family member or a teacher. Thousands of children phone helplines. Some phone the police. However, you might prefer to get advice on the internet. Always ask an adult to help you if you contact people on the internet.

Sharing your worries with a trusted person, such as a teacher, means that you do not need to cope on your own anymore.

# Help on the internet

You might choose to write messages on a website. The Hideout and ChildLine websites have message boards that allow you to write about different subjects, such as "Domestic violence – your views". Children write about their worries and experiences. You can make up a name and write **anonymously**. No one will know who you are. Experts will offer advice and answer any questions you have.

If you do not want to speak on a telephone, you can email many charities, such as Childline, for advice.

## Online!

You might be worried that the abuser will discover you are seeking help or talking about the abuse on your computer. However, nearly all websites that offer help on domestic violence give you instructions on covering your tracks. For example, the ChildLine website shows you how to hide the page immediately, in case the abuser comes into your room. It also explains how to stop the website appearing on the "history" of pages you have viewed. Abusers can become very angry if they know you are seeking help, so the instructions are worth following.

# Helplines

Children's **freephone** helplines such as ChildLine offer advice on domestic violence and other problems. Childline answers about 2,300 callers every day, and has counselled more than one million children since its helpline was set up in 1896.

The people who answer helplines are called **counsellors** and are specially trained to help you. They will not judge you and will not be shocked by anything you say. Most helplines promise to keep everything you say confidential, which means they will not pass on anything you have said to anyone else.

Specially trained counsellors answer the telephone calls to helplines such as ChildLine.

If someone is being attacked in their home, children often choose to phone the police.

## In an emergency

Even if you need to stop an attack in your home, you must stay safe yourself. It's not your responsibility to step in or risk getting hurt. In an emergency, if you can't get help from an adult such as a neighbour, call 999 and ask for the police. They will come quickly to help, at any time of day or night. They will make sure you are safe.

## CASE STUDY

Gracie's stepfather was often violent towards her mother. One day her stepfather slapped her mother so hard across the face that she fell on the floor. Her mother shouted to Gracie to run and call the police. Gracie ran next door, phoned the police and explained about the fight. The police had been to the house before. They came straight away and arrested Gracie's stepfather.

# Safe and cared for

It is often hard to leave an **abuser** but sometimes it is the best thing to do. Adults may decide to escape from their abuser by:

- leaving home. This might be just for a while or forever.
- getting the abuser to leave
- taking legal action against the abuser. This means using the law to force the abuser to stay away or to arrest the abuser to be tried in **court**.

Sometimes women feel so threatened by an abuser that they do not dare to go back home. They may be worried about the safety of their children, too.

# Getting away

If it is too dangerous to stay at home, a child or children and their mother may go to stay with relatives or friends, or go to a **refuge**. A family may have to take very few things with them and leave in a hurry before the abuser notices. If you think you might have to rush away suddenly with a parent, pack a small bag and hide it in a safe place. Include a favourite toy, such as a soft animal to cuddle.

# Locked doors

Some local authorities run "sanctuary schemes". The authorities pay someone to strengthen and add locks to one room in the victim's home. The victim and their family can then run into the room if an abuser who does not live in the same house is threatening them.

## WHAT DO YOU THINK?

Many children are upset that they must leave home to get away from an abusive relative. They may have to move to another part of the country and start a new school. Do you think this is the right thing to happen?

| Yes, the victim should move | No, the victim should stay |
| --- | --- |
| Moving away can be very upsetting, but it is the safest thing to do. | It is not fair that the victim has to move, the abuser should be made to move instead. |
| If the victim moves away somewhere secret, the abuser will not know where they are. The victim can live without fear. | The abuser should be arrested and sent to prison or be forced by law to stay away. |

# Where to go?

The safety and happiness of children is the most important issue in cases of domestic abuse. Getting away from the abuser is often the first, most important step. This may mean going to:

- a refuge or hostel
- a relative or friend's house
- a **children's home** or **foster home**.

Children may need to go to a children's home or foster home for a while if there isn't a parent, relative, or other **carer** to look after them.

# What is a refuge?

A refuge is a safe, secret house or hostel to escape to. Several mothers and children live in a refuge, and the refuge staff look after them. Staff might organize trips for the children and teenagers, such as to the cinema or shopping. However, sometimes the mothers or children are too nervous to go outside in case the abuser finds them.

## CASE STUDY

Children might feel sad to leave home and go to a refuge or move to another area. However, for many the feeling of safety outweighs the sadness. Here are some comments from children who have escaped from domestic violence:

"I feel safe now because I know no one can come and harm us." (9-year-old girl)

"Things couldn't be better. I'm not seeing all the things I used to see that I didn't want to. I hated seeing those things. And I'm seeing Mum being happy instead, and laughing." (16-year-old boy)

Children affected by domestic abuse may go to live for a while with other relatives, such as their grandparents.

## Taken into care

If your parents are cruel to you or **neglect** you, they may be sent to court. The court has the power to take you to live with people who can take better care of you. The court may ask the local authority to let you live with foster parents or in a children's home.

## A new life

A parent and his or her children may need to start a new life far away from the abuser. The children will have to go to a new school. These changes are worth it in the end, because they will help the family to be safe. The parent and children might all talk to a **counsellor**, who can help them cope better with painful memories of the abuse.

Talking to a trained counsellor helps children to start a new, happy life.

## CASE STUDY

Toby, aged 10, had to move house with his mother to get away from his dad. He felt much happier without his father around, and his mother smiled a lot more, too. Toby felt freer – he could relax at last and be himself. He felt safe knowing that if his dad found them, they could call for help. (Families are given emergency telephone numbers to ring to call for help if their abuser finds them.)

# What will happen to the abuser?

Group programmes or classes are run to help abusers. Trained group-workers encourage the abusers to talk through their feelings. The abusers learn how to notice when they are becoming abusive, and how to stop themselves. When possible, ex-abusers may be reunited with their family, or be able to see their children again.

Free from domestic violence, a family can rebuild their lives.

# Why does it happen?

If a parent, carer, or older relative is hurting you, then remember that you are not to blame. It is not your fault. Many **victims** believe they have caused the problems that led to the domestic violence, but they have not.

**Abusers** are often driven by a wish to have power and control. Other things can contribute to abusive behaviour, but do not cause it by themselves. Some of these things are:

- alcohol
- drugs
- unemployment
- stress
- ill health
- past experiences, such as being **abused** themselves.

All of these problems can be solved with determination and help, such as counselling. Most people can cope with these problems without becoming an abuser.

## CASE STUDY

An abuser will often blame the victim for what is happening, but there is never any excuse for being violent. This 12-year-old boy's dad tried to blame his mum. He remembers how this made him feel confused: "I don't know [whose fault it was]. My dad used to say it was my mum's. I don't know why, but I believed him, and then I didn't know who to believe. ... I didn't know who to choose. But I think it was my dad's fault really." It is confusing when both parents blame each other for violence. But remember what abuse is and it will become clear which parent is the abuser. Keeping this clear in your mind will help you cope.

Alcohol and other problems can influence people's behaviour. Alcohol can make people more aggressive.

# Forced marriages

In some cultures, parents arrange a marriage, matching their child with a partner. If the marriage is against the will of one or both people, it is a forced marriage. Forced marriages are seen as a form of abuse by many governments and by the **United Nations**.

Children are sometimes forced to return to their parents' native country to marry. If you are frightened of being forced into a marriage, talk to a teacher at school or phone a **helpline**.

Some people believe that children can get married at the age of 12. This is illegal in Western countries, where 18 (or 16 with parents' agreement) is the most common legal age.

# Repeating patterns?

Why do certain people become abusers? In some cases, it may be to do with the abuser's need to control other people. Other times the abuser is repeating an experience they themselves had as a child. Most adults who are abusive were abused themselves as children. However, most children who are abused do not grow up to be abusive adults. Counselling helps children who have experienced domestic abuse to go on to live very happy lives.

## BEHIND THE HEADLINES

In 2010 two brothers aged 10 and 11 from Edlington, South Yorkshire were imprisoned for brutally torturing two young children, nearly killing one of them. The brothers had **witnessed** domestic abuse, and one brother was shown violent videos from an early age. A lawyer described their family life as "toxic". However, the judge decided that the boys had to be kept away from society because of their dangerous behaviour.

This picture was drawn during the Edlington brothers' **court** case. The boys' faces were not drawn, to protect their identities.

# Brave first step

Domestic violence is a terrible experience – whether you are a witness or the victim. But as we have seen, there are ways of coping and there are many caring people who want to help you. Reaching out for help becomes easier after the first step has been made. The first brave phone call to a helpline or a chat to an adult you trust can change everything. Remembering that many other children have experienced the same thing helps too. Reading their stories on websites such as The Hideout (see page 47) can be **inspiring** and comforting.

# Awareness

It can take time to move away from domestic violence. Everyone in the home has to be aware of what is going on. The victims and witnesses must understand that it is not their fault, and that they should get help.

# Rebuilding lives

Once a family or children have escaped from abuse, they can rebuild their lives. It can take time to cope with the past. Children sometimes find it helpful to paint pictures or write about what happened to them. Talking about feelings and supporting your family will make you all feel happier. Don't forget to give a few hugs to those you love.

# Online!

Look through some of the recommended contacts on pages 46–47. If possible, ask a trusted adult to help you research domestic violence using the websites listed. Knowing and understanding more about domestic violence makes it easier to cope with it.

After escaping from domestic violence, a parent might find a new, kind partner with whom everyone feels safe.

# Top ten tips for coping with domestic violence

Dealing with domestic violence is often difficult, but you can overcome **abuse**. Here are some tips to help you cope as you look towards a new life:

1.  Remember that there is no excuse for domestic violence. It should never happen. No matter what an **abuser** might say, it is wrong.

2.  After experiencing abuse, find a quiet, safe place where you can calm down and think carefully about what to do.

3.  Remember that domestic violence is never your fault.

4.  Talk to an adult you can trust, such as a parent, other relative, teacher, neighbour, or friend of your parents. Tell them what is happening. They should support you and be there when you need them. They will help you get practical help too, and more information on what to do.

5.  Call a **helpline** (see pages 46–47). The people who answer will be caring and sensitive. They will have the knowledge and experience to be able to help you.

6.  In an emergency, phone 999 and ask for the police, or ask an adult to phone them for you.

7.  If you are planning to run away, ring a helpline first, such as ChildLine. They will help you.

8.  Look at children's websites for advice and information. You can get personal advice by emailing or messaging the websites (see pages 46–47 for the addresses).

9.   If you are feeling angry, upset, or unhappy, try some of these ideas: write a diary, find an empty space such as a field and scream, cry, draw a picture, ring a friend, or talk to an adult you can trust. Remember that it is okay to feel strong emotions.

10.  Always remember that help is waiting for you. You can find confidential help on the telephone any time, day or night.

Writing about your feelings in a diary can help you to work things out. If you later read through what you have written, you might be able to come up with solutions to any problems.

# Glossary

**abuse**  harm or cruelty

**abuser**  person who harms or hurts someone repeatedly

**anonymously**  with no one knowing your name. If you talk anonymously, no one knows it is you talking.

**assault**  illegal attack on someone, which may harm the victim

**carer**  anyone who looks after someone else in the home, such as a parent or a trained worker in a children's home

**child abuse**  harm that is done repeatedly to a child, ranging from neglect to hitting

**children's home**  home for children whose parents are unable to look after them. Children may stay in a children's home for a short time while waiting to return to their parents or to be found a foster home.

**counsellor**  person who has been trained to give advice or to guide people as they make decisions and try to cope with life

**court**  place where a judge makes legal decisions. People who have broken the law go to court for a trial.

**criminal offence**  act that can be punished by law.  Punching someone is a criminal offence.

**emotional**  to do with feelings or emotions, and having strong feelings. Victims of abuse often feel emotional.

**foster home**  family that offers a home to children who need one. Staying in a foster home is like living with a new family.

**freephone**  telephone number that does not cost anything to call

**helpline** (sometimes called hotline) telephone service offering advice. Helplines are often free.

**inspiring** giving encouragement or new ideas

**isolate** keep someone away from other people so that they cannot see or talk to others

**neglect** lack of care. Child neglect can mean that a child is not given enough love, food, education, warmth, or safety.

**ongoing** continuing. Ongoing abuse does not stop – it keeps happening.

**physical** to do with the body. If someone hits you, that is physical abuse.

**refuge** safe house or hostel for abused women and children to escape to

**self-esteem** a person's belief in their own worth and abilities

**sexual** to do with sex, and the private parts of your body, or the private parts of another person's body

**United Nations** worldwide organization concerned with world peace, security, and human rights

**unlawful imprisonment** locking someone up against their will, and which therefore breaks the law

**verbal** spoken or said. Verbal abuse involves shouting or saying words that hurt, upset, or frighten the listener.

**victim** person who is hurt by someone else

**witness** person who sees or hears something happen

# Find out more

## Books

*Divorce and Separation (Tough Topics)*, Patricia Murphy (Heinemann Library, 2008)

*Violent Feelings (Choices and Decisions)*, Pete Sanders and Steve Myers (Franklin Watts, 2007)

*When Parents Separate (Choices and Decisions)*, Pete Sanders and Steve Myers (Franklin Watts, 2007)

## Websites and organizations

The following organizations and websites can offer help and support to you and your family:

**Barnardo's**
www.barnardos.org.uk/fosteringandadoption.htm
Barnardo's is a nationwide organization that helps children to cope with family changes such as being fostered or adopted.

**ChildLine**
www.childline.org.uk
Helpline: 0800 1111
ChildLine has trained counsellors who give advice, support, and information on a range of issues. Calls are free and won't appear on the phone bill. Visit their website to find out how to email their counsellors or chat to them online. You can also write to ChildLine at Freepost 1111, London, N1 0BR (no stamp needed).

**Convention on the Rights of the Child**
www.unicef.org.uk/tz/resources/assets/pdf/
every_child_colour_leaflet.pdf
Find out about your rights in this leaflet made by UNICEF.

### The Hideout
www.thehideout.org.uk
This website has lots of information on domestic violence, what it is like to stay in a refuge, and children's stories about how they have coped with domestic violence. There is also a message board you can join to talk about any problems you are having.

### National Association for Children of Alcoholics (Nacoa)
www.nacoa.org.uk
Helpline: 0800 358 3456
Email: helpline@nacoa.org.uk
You can telephone or email the Nacoa helpline for advice and support if your parent has a drink problem.

### Refuge
www.refuge.org.uk
Helpline: 0808 2000 247
This website and helpline offers advice to women and children affected by domestic abuse, and explains all about staying in a refuge.

### Runaway Helpline
Telephone: 0808 800 7070
This is free helpline you can call for help and advice if you are thinking of running away, or have run away.

### The Safe Space
www.thesafespace.org/the-basics
You can look on this website for information and advice if you are worried about dating violence, or if you feel like someone is using a mobile phone to control you.

# Index